A LIFETIME OF
COLLECTING EXPERIENCES

A Memoir by Paul Hickey

NIGHT
RIVER
PRESS

For permission requests, write to the publisher, addressed "Attention: Permissions Coordinator," at the address below.

Night River Press Denver, CO 80209
www.NightRiverPress.com
Skeetieb@me.com

ISBN: 978-0-9964349-6-6 (Paperback)
ISBN: 978-0-9964349-7-3 (eBook)
ISBN: 978-0-9964349-8-0 (Hard Cover)

Any references to historical events, real people, or real places are used fictitiously. Names, characters, and places are products of the author's imagination.

Book cover and interior design by Susan Malikowski
Cover Photo by Nicole Wickens
Book edited by Victoria Walker

Printed by Night River Press LLC, in the United States of America
First printing edition 2021.

This book is dedicated to Lisa Hickey Baile for her assistance and sharp eye with proofreading and suggesting improvements to this manuscript.

Contents

CONTENTS

CHAPTER ONE

The Green Shawl

During the Irish Potato Famine in the late 1840s, my maternal great-grandfather, John Clancy, immigrated to central Kentucky and acquired a farm.

John came to the United States from County Clare, Ireland, with his brother, Tim, and his friend, Patrick Loughlin. (The Clancys were stonemasons and found work building brick and stone chimneys, stone walls, and general roadwork.) John prepared for his wife and children to join him.

My great-grandmother, Mary Elizabeth Murphy Clancy, took an immigrant ship from Ireland to New Orleans to rejoin her husband. En route, her youngest baby girl got a high fever, which was not tolerated back then because she could have sickened the crew and other passengers. If discovered, she would have been thrown overboard. Mary Elizabeth spent much of the Atlantic crossing with her sick baby girl hidden under her green shawl whenever any crewman walked by.

Her husband was to meet her in New Orleans but when she arrived he was not at the dock to greet her. She searched the rooming houses where the Irish would have been expected to stay and could not find him. So she placed her belongings in storage and checked into a boarding house to wait for him. Time passed and then she found out the storage building where her baggage was stored had burned down and she had lost all of her possessions. Her brother-in-law, Tim, found her and told her that her husband had died of typhoid while waiting for her arrival.

Mary Elizabeth and her children, together with Tim and his Irish friend, Patrick, rented a horse and wagon to return to the farm in Kentucky. I heard through family lore that she had her husband's body exhumed from its above-ground burial site in New Orleans so she could take him to Kentucky for his final resting place, but I cannot confirm this.

They traveled up the Natchez Trace to Louisville. They continued to the Carlisle area and ultimately settled the family near Mount Sterling, Kentucky. At some point Mary and Patrick got married, despite her being significantly older than him.

The baby girl that almost died was my grandmother, Margaret Clancy. She lived a happy and long life; she was 84 when she passed away and I was about seven. There is no doubt I come from a long line of strong women. Had it not been for the love and courage of my great-grandmother, and that green shawl, my life story that you are about to read would not have come to pass.

CHAPTER TWO

Where it All Began

Born at the very beginning of the Great Depression, I was the youngest of seven children. At that time, my father was a farmer, raising tobacco and living in a tenant house with no electricity and no running water. It was about one mile away from the nearest paved road.

When I was about ten, our house burned down and destroyed all of our possessions. The fire occurred when we were at school so I'm not sure how it started. We didn't have insurance—it had run out the month before. For an interim period, we moved to another tenant house on the same farm. This house also burned down.

The economy was such that banks were lending money to trustworthy people such as my dad to cover the full purchase price on a home. That is when we bought the exceptionally nice house with 83 acres on Donaldson Road. I was in 6th grade and it was here that we first had electricity and running water. We finally lived on the paved road.

These were trying financial years and my father showed a tremendous amount of ingenuity in keeping us solvent. This included shipping horses in from Montana, where two of his siblings had homesteaded. He would get the wild horses from the ranches and public lands, where they were very cheap. Then he hired cowboys to care for them en route. They would gather up the horses and put them in railroad cars. My dad and the hired cowboys would travel in the train's caboose.

Dad now had horses galore and lots of cowboys so he put the two together and decided to hold rodeos in small towns around central Kentucky. We learned there were two types of rodeo cowboys: the permanent ones who would live on our farm in the barn and those just passing through, having heard about the potential for prize money. Some would come in from Oklahoma and other Western states for the rodeo. They often adopted colorful names; I remember a redhead from Nevada who called himself Red Reno.

During one rodeo in Mount Sterling, Dad gave me a pistol, a bag and the gate take. (The gate take was the cash from admission fees.) Dad told me to protect that money no matter what. I knew how to shoot a pistol but luckily no one tried to get into the locked car during the time I was guarding it. I think I was eight.

The highlights of a small town rodeo were the bull riding, bucking horses, and barrel races for the competing cowgirls. My brother Jim, when he was well beyond rodeo days and had already been through college and the Navy, was with his wife Frances. They were going to a rodeo and he told her he used to do bull riding when he was a teenager. Behind his back, she registered him to ride in the event. For the sake of his pride, he had to compete and got on the bull. He was about 35 but he could still stay on the bull.

Joe Komarek was the main cowboy we dealt with back then. He was on our payroll because he lived at our house and would help break horses for Dad. Years later, Judy and I visited him on his large ranch in Roy, Montana. He instantly was attracted to Judy and offered her a plot of scenic land if she would like to build a vacation house there.

It was said that the cowboys would pay the Indians to drive their own horses across the river from the reservation so they could be intermingled with the wild horses. Dad would buy the horses, break them, and then sell them as workhorses.

Interestingly, the depression helped the horse-trading business. The use of tractors in the farming industry was well underway by then but the depression made it impractical to use tractors because of the expense of fuel. Since horses simply ate grass and hay, farmers went back to using them for farm work.

In addition to raising tobacco and putting on rodeos, my dad was also a horse and cattle trader. He would buy anything and sell it at a profit. My dad was very clever and he was gifted at math and doing equations quickly in his head. He had a fantastic reputation.

My typical day on the farm was to wake up before dawn and head to the barn to milk the cows. Sometimes, we would let the cows stay in the field overnight and on those mornings I would get up even earlier to find the cows in the field and herd them back to the barn. We usually had about 12 milk cows and I would milk half of them and our work hand would milk the rest.

We'd put the milk in eight-gallon milk cans and put them near the road if it was pick-up day, when one of the large milk companies such as Carnation would get the fresh milk from participating farmers. It was a secondary source of income for us.

We would store the filled milk buckets in our spring-house. This was an enclosed stone building over our spring that was used for natural refrigeration. The spring on our farm was unique because it was known as bottom-less; no one could ever find the bottom of it. I'd put a weight on the end of a rope and still never found the bottom. During periods of drought, our neighbors would bring their water tanks and wagons and fill them up with the cold, clear water.

With my morning chores done, I would get washed up and dressed for school. My mother would cook a hearty breakfast of eggs, ham, bacon, toast and cereal. Afterward, she would head to the front porch to "sweep" when the bus was expected. She would call me when the bus was there or stop the bus driver from driving off.

When I got back home from school, I would milk the cows again—you milked them twice a day. I then had to churn the butter. I also worked with the tobacco or the horses. There were always chores to do on the farm. I worked all the time.

When I was about twelve, Dad told me he would match any money that I saved and I could put it toward paying for college. This motivated me to take as many jobs as possible, even if they were low paying. I would cut weeds on our neighbor's farm for $2 a day. Dad invested my savings in cattle and then doubled my money, helping me to pay for the last few years of college.

The way you eat on a farm is a lot different from how you eat in the city, a lesson I learned the hard way. With farm work, you get a real appetite. We would have three proper meals a day—breakfast, dinner and supper. Supper was the more formal meal and we would eat together as a family. At every meal, we would typically have three meats—ham, bacon, shoulder, chicken, or beef.

I got fired from a job as a restaurant worker in Cincinnati for eating too much. It was an upscale restaurant and I was working there during my freshman year of college. After each shift, you could sit down and eat a free meal. I would order steak and ham and usually a third meat, with a few sides. They fired me and said it was too expensive to feed me. I thought everyone ate like that.

CHAPTER THREE

Siblings

King was the third oldest and he was the family celebrity for a number of reasons. He was very smart and studious. Whatever he did, he tried to do it well. He was a perfectionist. He matured early and was in college at age sixteen, which is why he was commissioned into the military so young for World War II. He was one of the first people to complete his maximum number of bombing raids in the war and then came back to train others in the U.S. After getting his law degree, he was the Executive Director of the Attorney General Association in Lexington. He was also the Director of Continuing Education for the University of Kentucky. He married and had three children.

My sister Florence was the oldest. She had a great

sense of humor and immense raw intelligence. She started out as a schoolteacher before becoming a principal and then was second-in-line to the superintendent of schools in Lexington. She worked hard for low-income students by applying for grants for them through the federal and state government.

Christine was the second oldest and was a flight nurse in WWII. Later, she was the head nurse at the University of Kentucky healthcare center and then the head nurse at the Army Signal Depot in Avon. She was a natural diagnostician and was very well respected. She provided home care to both Mother and Dad during their final years.

Mary Catherine (Cat) had no fear of anything. On her little farm outside New Albany, Indiana, when she was in her 60s, she was tending her garden when two burglars did not notice she was there and started to head toward her back door. She challenged them, told them to stop but they ignored her. She reached into her nearby purse and pulled out a pistol. "Get down on your knees," she said. "You wouldn't shoot us, old lady," one of them chuckled. Without skipping a beat, with the pistol pointed at him, she said, "Make my day!" There was a feature article about it in a Louisville newspaper, calling her a "pistol-packing senior." This instance characterizes Cat's approach to life.

Jim was five years older than me. He had a strong sense of humor and never seemed to worry about anything. (He caused other people to worry.) I spent a lot of summers with Jim during my college years and we had a lot of fun adventures. He married and lived in Montana and had four children.

Dorothy (Dot) was two years older than me and truly everybody loved Dot. After she graduated from high school, she went to Montana to see relatives. She met Larry Wickens, who was recently out of the military, and they fell in love and got married quickly, not having known each other very long. Dot told us they were driving to Great Falls to buy her a wedding ring when she thought to herself, "I don't even know this man and I am about to marry him." They settled into his ranch outside of Winifred, Montana, and raised six children.

CHAPTER FOUR

The Matriarch: Aunt Bridgie

The matriarch of the Hickey family was Bridget Hickey, better known as Aunt Bridgie. She stayed active until she died at 106, weeks from her 107th birthday. She had never been in a hospital until she got pneumonia and died. She was very social and liked to cook and entertain. She kept up with current affairs and was very interested in world events. Our large extended family would meet at her house after church on Sunday mornings.

Bridget and her sister, Josie, were two of the early female homesteaders in Montana. It was unheard of back then for an unmarried woman to apply for and get land but they did it. Aunt Bridgie never married. She was a schoolteacher in Oklahoma, Kentucky, and Montana.

Josie was in her 60s when she married Uncle Ed Jones, who was a mailman and undertaker in Roy, Montana.

At Aunt Bridgie's 95th birthday party on the farm, someone suggested they saddle up a horse so she could go for a ride since she had always loved horses. She thought it was a good idea and was enjoying her ride. Jim walked around the corner of the house with a shotgun in his hand. Without warning, he raised it and shot at the tree branch above her head. A large snake fell to the ground next to her horse. "Good shot, Jim," she calmly said.

CHAPTER FIVE

The Road to Knowledge

My parents were the driving force behind education for their children. They had both been schoolteachers, as it seems was everyone else in the family for at least some amount of time. My mother was very bright. She played the piano and was very well read. She insisted that all of us get an education. All of my siblings went to college except for Cat and Dot, who got married young. Out of seven children, there were a total of ten college or advanced degrees.

I went to Sideview Public School from 1st–4th grade. Florence had taught there for some years. My teacher, Miss Mark, was absolutely top notch. I used to say I was the teacher's pet because she couldn't afford a dog.

After we moved, I attended Wadesmill School in Clark County for one year. In sixth grade, I started at St. Agatha Academy, a private Catholic school in Winchester. I was the only one of my siblings who went to Catholic school and I was there for six years. The rest of the family went to Mount Sterling High School or Winchester High School. Our farm was at the intersection of three counties so we could choose our high school. Florence, King and Christine went to Mount Sterling. Catherine, Dot and Jim went to Winchester.

I was usually the only country boy at St. Agatha. To pay for tuition, my dad bartered farm produce with the nuns. The teachers were Sisters of Divine Providence. The parish did not own the school; it was independent. A number of students were not Catholic and attended for a quality education. They usually returned to the public school for their senior year so their degree would reflect this. I believe I received a solid education.

I graduated as the valedictorian of my class in 1947. My classmate and very good friend, John Collis, was the salutatorian and he went on to become a brain surgeon in Cleveland, Ohio. I received four-year scholarships to both Villa Madonna College in Covington and Kentucky Wesleyan College in Winchester. I went to both of those colleges for one year each and then transferred to the University of Kentucky, where I graduated in 1952 with majors in English and History.

Around the time I graduated high school, I decided I would collect experiences. This made me determined to visit as many cities, states, and countries that I could. I think I succeeded with that goal.

CHAPTER SIX

Following the Wheat Harvest

During my first summer break at college, I followed the wheat harvest to make money. Operating tractors, trucks, and combines, I worked in the Dakotas, Montana, Kansas, and Nebraska. The last summer I did this, I was with my brother Jim and Matt Anderson, a Winchester friend. We started down south in Kansas and worked our way up the Great Plains states to Montana.

To find work, you'd drive up the road and see a large ripening wheat field. You could either stop and knock on the door of the farmer's house and ask if they needed workers or enquire with the local agencies to help find work. Once you got hired, you would sleep in a bed in the bunkhouse and the housewife would prepare food for the workers. The farmer would decide which piece of equipment you would handle. You could be the truck driver and haul the wheat to the grain elevators or, if you were more experienced, you could drive the combine that cuts and thrashes the wheat.

The days were long, at least 10 hours of work a day. We had to get up early to beat the weather. You can't cut damp wheat so the sun would have to be out. We would usually stay a week to get it done. It was worth it because we got twice as much money as we would have been paid working in Kentucky, which was generally $5/day. Here, we were making $10-15/day per person. Sometimes the locals didn't like us because we'd go into the bars and dance with their women. There were often fights. I was glad to have Jim there, as he always won.

CHAPTER SEVEN

Boxing and Fighting

Growing up, Jim, King, and I had boxing gloves. Jim was Kentucky's first runner-up in the Golden Gloves competition. Jim got a lot of coverage in the local papers. They called him the "Smiling Irishman" because he was always smiling even as he would beat up his opponent. When they were younger, my older brother King had always beat Jim during their boxing matches. Then, when Jim was about 18, King realized Jim had grown larger and stronger and he was wise enough to never fight him again.

Back in high school, I was in the most publicized fight in Winchester. Spec Lacy had a reputation for being the toughest kid in town. He went to the public school while I was at St. Agatha. He wanted to fight me and so we started to fight outside. The school coach heard the commotion and came over and broke it up. He said, "Let's make this a real fight." So he moved us into the Winchester High School gym and gave us boxing gloves. The auditorium filled up with people. Spec didn't whip me and I didn't beat him. The coach called it a draw. We later became friends.

Spec (Ronald) Lacy went on to become a professional bodybuilder and won Mr. Kentucky in 1955. In 1957, he was Mr. America and later won 1st place as Mr. Universe in his height category. After he became famous, he opened a body building gym in Winchester. Our Austin neighbor who was from Kentucky, Lou Hornung, knew Spec Lacy and had worked out at his gym in Winchester. Lou was in awe that I had achieved a draw in a fight with Spec.

CHAPTER EIGHT

One-Room Schoolhouse

In the middle of college, I stayed out for a year and taught school in a one-room schoolhouse in Fergus County, Montana, north of Lewistown. I did this to replenish my cash reserves to afford the remainder of college. It was probably the only school in the country that had eight grades and only two students. The students were neighbors and one lived within walking distance and the other lived about two miles from the school. He had to cross a mountain range and would come on horseback or by tractor.

There was electricity but no running water, therefore no indoor plumbing. One of the students would bring me a bucket of water every day. I would ask for two buckets, if needed.

The school had a basement with a bed in it that was designed to be the teacher's living quarters. But I chose not to sleep there when I found out the previous teacher had died in the bed two years earlier and it had not been cleaned since. (There was no school for two years since they couldn't find a teacher until I came along.) I decided to put the mattress on the floor of the upstairs clothes closet because the basement creeped me out. I cooked over a kerosene hot plate and the building was heated by a single potbelly stove.

Nothing prepared me for that frigid cold winter and this happened to be a record-setting year. I remember waking up many times and my breath had frozen to the blanket. I would have to shake myself loose to get out and start a fire in the stove and jump back under the covers, shivering until the stove started to produce heat. There was no bathroom and no insulation. The single-pane windows had many crevices that the wind could blow through.

On the bright side, to clean the schoolhouse, all I had to do was sweep snow into the room, stir it around and then sweep it all out. The floor went from snow white to coal black. The snow would pick up all of the dirt.

One weekend when there was a heavy snowstorm, I was driving to visit my sister Dot and her husband, Larry, on their ranch. The roads are built so they are higher than the surrounding ground, allowing the wind to blow the snow off the road. The road to Suffolk is elevated high enough to not have snow build up. When I turned off that road toward the ranch, the road was elevated but there were still snow banks. When I turned toward the gate, basically a wire contraption, I careened off the road and the car got stuck. I had to walk about a mile to their house. The snow had frozen on top so you would fall through the ice down into the snow with each step, making it difficult to walk. Plus, the temperature was about 30 below.

I finally made it to Dot and Larry's house and asked Larry to go back with me in his Caterpillar tractor to pull my car out of the snow. He got all of the proper equipment and we drove back toward my car.

I had always heard that drinking whiskey would keep you from freezing so I had buried a bottle of whiskey in the snow bank right near the gate so I could find it. I spotted my car and jumped out of the tractor. As I passed the gate, I remembered the bottle of whiskey, reached into the snow bank and retrieved it. I unplugged the cork, raised the bottle to take a big swig, thinking it would help me better tolerate the cold.

I thought Larry had gone crazy. He jumped off the tractor and slapped the bottle out of my hand, where it emptied in the snow. "If you had drank that, you would be dead," he said.

Having grown up in the South, I had no idea of the peculiarities of below zero weather. Larry explained, "Remember, many liquids like water freeze at 32 degrees. Alcohol does not. The liquor was not frozen even though the temperature was the same as the outside at 30 below. As soon as that touched your stomach, your stomach would freeze."

I had no idea of such things. He saved my life, despite my ignorance. I quickly became more knowledgeable about living in freezing cold weather.

CHAPTER NINE

Cuba

After teaching in Montana, I transferred to the University of Kentucky for my last two years of college. During spring break of my junior year, I took a memorable trip to Cuba in 1951. I had been living in a first-floor room in the army barracks that had been converted into dorms for U.K. college students. Every morning I awoke to loud crashing noises coming from the room above me. I couldn't take it any longer so I went upstairs to set the occupant straight. I pounded on the door. When the door opened, I was looking at a body builder with rippling muscles. He would lift weights early every morning and he'd drop them on his floor/my ceiling.

This is how I met my soon-to-be travel companion

and this is when he made me an offer. He told me he had just completed his military service and with the money he received, he had bought a new Mercury. He said that if I find four paying passengers, then I could get a free ride to Florida.

The driver turned out to be dumb as a rock. He wouldn't let anyone else drive his car and he was a terrible driver. He also always had to be in charge. By the time we got to Miami, all of the paid passengers rebelled and just wanted to get away from him. They all got out in Miami.

He and I continued south to Key West. There, we discovered cheap flights by nonscheduled airlines to Cuba for something like $30. The days and times were not announced until they got enough passengers to fly.

My first experience in Havana was when we were getting our checked baggage. All of the other experienced travelers waved money at the attendant to bribe him to get their luggage. All bags were gone from the conveyer belt except for ours. The bus to go downtown was waiting for us and wouldn't wait any longer. On principle, my travel companion refused to pay a bribe for our bags. He dragged the attendant across the conveyer belt and threatened him to get his bag, which by the way was extremely heavy. It turns out he had packed his barbells and no change of clothes, only a few T-shirts.

That set the tone for our relationship in Cuba. We found a cheap hotel and had an evening that I won't describe except to say I spent all my money except for three Cuban cents. Of course, my companion wouldn't loan me any money. He did agree to buy me food but he would determine what he would buy and how much of it. I ended up eating free samples of cheese and rum given to tourists at liquor stores. I tried to fly back but the nonscheduled airlines had no set return flight. (That is why they were so inexpensive.) We subsequently stayed several extra days in Havana, waiting for a flight.

One of the trip highlights was that there was a large parade with the President. He was standing in a convertible. A large crowd followed him chanting, "El Presidente es mal y Batista es bueno!" On a side note, soon there was a coup that overthrew the president and installed Fulgencio Batista.

Many years later, I went to a party in Havana that was hosted by Batista for U.S. Navy officers who were in port. (This was a few months before Castro took over.) It was the most extravagant party I have ever attended. We wore dress whites, an impressive uniform not often seen. Each naval officer had his own personal waiter serving them drinks. They had poured cement over a soccer field to create a stage for the band and imported Spanish flamenco dancers for entertainment.

After the party, three of us went downtown to the Florida Bar. It was nearly empty except for the staff and a couple sitting at a dark corner table. We settled at the bar and a waiter came over to us and said, "Señor Hemingway and his wife are seated over there and would like for you to come join them for a drink."

Our executive officer, Red Youman, was a noticeably big, loud guy with bright red hair. Without missing a beat, Red said to the waiter, "If he wants to drink with us, he will come over here." Needless to say, we didn't have the drink with Ernest Hemingway.

Back to my earlier story about Cuba, I finally located a flight to Florida and had to borrow the money from my travel companion. We had to hurry to get to the airport to catch the flight. We hopped in a cab and agreed on a price. After driving to random places, the driver said he was lost and it would cost more money. For the first time, I appreciated my travel companion. He grabbed the driver at his throat and dragged him across the seat. He told him that if we miss our plane, he would break his back. The cab driver immediately drove us directly to the airport.

We made it to Miami and met up with the other passengers to drive back to Kentucky. The problem now was my travel companion was the worst driver on the face of the earth. He drove down the white stripe in the middle of the road and every car we met was a potential accident. He got meaner and meaner during the trip. He was just dumb and domineering. When we were about 30 miles outside of Lexington, he ran another car off the road and caused an accident. All of the other passengers agreed to find another way home. I paid him back all of the money I owed him and never saw him again.

I did end up visiting Havana multiple times again and frequently went in and out of Guantanamo Bay Naval Base throughout my time in the Navy.

CHAPTER TEN

Alaska

During the following summer, I took an unintentional trip to Alaska. I started off hitchhiking to Montana to work on the Wickens' ranch for a few months. One of the early rides I caught was with a man driving alone in a very expensive car. He soon asked me if I had a driver's license. If so, he asked if I would drive the car for a while. It turned out he was testing me to see if I would help him to herd a small fleet of used cars that he was supervising in route to Seattle.

He had gathered up a group of primarily young, wild drivers following him in his cars. He needed help keeping them in line and making sure none of them left the caravan to steal a car.

Immediately, I knew I could help him. I noticed that when refueling the cars, he was randomly stopping at regular gas stations and paying full price for the gas. I asked for his permission to handle the next fuel stop. He agreed. At the next stop, I spoke with the gas station manager and got his agreement to charge the truck price per gallon—trucks received a substantial discount—for all ten cars we had in our group. He was pleased when I saved him money and agreed to pay all of my expenses, including all hotels and restaurants.

When we reached southern Montana and I was to get out, he said I could continue on with him to Seattle. I decided to change my plans and head to the West Coast. King and Betty lived in Tacoma on an Air Force base so I thought I would visit them.

I was about thirty miles away from King and Betty's house when I hitched another ride with a young man, who was driving a top-of-the-line new Ford sporty car with a continental tire on the back. This was the sharpest thing going in those days. He told me he was an Alaskan from Fairbanks and he had come down to buy his new car and drive it back. He said I could join him on the drive to Alaska and share gas expenses if I wanted. I immediately agreed. So I had a brief visit with King and Betty and joined him on his drive back to Alaska.

We had to go east toward Idaho to pick up the AL-CAN (Alaska-Canadian) Highway. It was built during World War II to connect the contiguous United States to Alaska and it had only opened up to the public a few years earlier. Once in Canada, the driver wanted to stop in every city because he had never traveled before. I was running out of money. When we finally got to White-horse, the capital of the Yukon Territory, we found the road was impassable due to a landslide. So we had to drive back to Whitehorse and wait it out there for several days, watching as the population expanded daily due to the highway closure.

It was the Fourth of July and some of us Americans were celebrating beyond the Mounties' tolerance. One colorful traveler informed the Canadians that they would cause an international incident if they continued to quell our patriotic festivities.

At this point, I completely ran out of money. People were generous with food so I wasn't facing starvation.

The prices were much more expensive than in the States. I wired my sisters, Florence and Christine, asking if they would send me money. Days went by and no response. Finally, on the day the road opened up and all of the truckers and travelers were leaving town, the money order came through and I was financed. Shortly after leaving Whitehorse, we entered the Alaskan territory and the remainder of the driving trip was uneventful.

I got a job working for a construction company in Fairbanks and slept in a tent with six other people, paying nominal rent. There were two military sites that the company had a contract with to pack and ship officers' belongings back to the States. I passed myself off as a carpenter, saying I grew up on a farm and built barns. The other people on the crew were very impressive contractors, who could drive five nails to my one. The job was to nail shut the shipping cartons that held the officer's possessions. The first time I felt the nail drive into something hard, I realized it was being driven into the furniture stored in the box. I was immediately released by mutual consent of the other co-workers. There was not ill will; they were just concerned that my nails would fly like missiles and hit someone.

I was job hunting again and found work more suited to my qualifications. It was with a large company that was constructing new buildings on an Air Force base. They hired me as a truck driver. With great luck, one of the managers was from Central Montana near my sister and he gave me the cushiest job, driving the bus that took the workers to and from the building site and the tent area. During the day, I ran the water truck to bring drinking water to the workers and to water the cement to cure. It was a seven-day-a-week job and I made good money— multiple of what I would have made in Montana, which was about $10/day. In Alaska, I was making $63/day.

The workers were very interesting people who followed job opportunities around the world. They were largely Americans. I remember there were a few professional gamblers, who were successful at getting money from the workers. They always won. I did partake in gambling but I quickly learned that I wasn't any good at it. This was during the summer months so there was no darkness. The sun would dip below the horizon but it didn't turn dark.

We had a real nasty supervisor. He had ordered a new station wagon from the States to be delivered to him in Alaska and it had taken over a month to arrive. He was the only person with a new car. One memorable experience involved a man who was a crane operator and his friend who was the rigger—the one who stood on the ground giving directions. One afternoon, the dislikable supervisor came speeding over to them and slammed on the brakes and jumped out of his new station wagon, cursing and confusing the crane operator.

Very quietly, the rigger waved directions to the crane operator to line up the crane on the edge of the pit in alignment with the supervisor's new station wagon that was on the other side of the pit. The rigger made the signal to drive forward, having the crane fall into the pit and chop the station wagon in two. The supervisor was speechless. There was nothing he could do about it. Calmly, the crane operator told the incredulous supervisor that he and the rigger were resigning for better opportunities elsewhere and they got out of there as fast as possible.

When it was time to head back to college, I found a nonscheduled flight on a C-47, going from Fairbanks to Seattle, with a fueling stop in Anchorage. Once in Seattle, I hitchhiked during the day and slept on the bus at night to get back to college in Kentucky.

World War II

From the time we moved to Donaldson Road in 1938 until the war was imminent, most of my siblings were in college. It was only Dot, Jim and I living at home. When we entered the war in 1941, all of my five siblings who were old enough to go to war, did so.

King had a head start because he was in ROTC in college and was deployed with the early American airmen in the war. King was a bombardier in the B-17 fleet bombers in the Air Corps in Europe. He completed his maximum bombing flights at an early stage and returned to the States and trained. At the war's end, he returned to civilian life and got his law degree from the University of Kentucky. He returned to the military with JAG—

the Judge Advocate General's Corps.

Florence joined the WAVES as an enlisted person and was involved in secret classified work in New York City and Washington, D.C. She was never allowed to talk about it.

Christine, who we later called Ann, joined the Army Air Corps as a nurse and served in the Pacific. She was actively involved in most major engagements in the Pacific Islands. She'd fly into the active fighting. The plane would land and they would load as many injured as possible and fly back out.

Jim joined the Navy as a bosun mate on a Destroyer Escort (DE), a small version of a destroyer that was highly maneuverable and fitted with sonar, radar, and weapons. He served in South America and elsewhere. He got out of the Navy at the end of the war and then got his college degree and returned to the Navy until the end of the Korean War.

During this time, children were expected to do their share for the war effort. This included scrap metal drives, collecting rubber, traveling by bike or horseback to save petrol, and doing the farm chores of milking and feeding livestock while older siblings were away.

At that time, you couldn't just walk into a shop and buy as much sugar, butter or meat as you wanted nor could you fill up your car with gasoline whenever you liked. All of these things were rationed, which meant you were only allowed to buy a small amount, even if you could afford more. The government introduced rationing because certain things were in short supply during the war and rationing was the only way to make sure everyone got their fair share.

Serving as a U.S. Naval Officer

When I got out of college, Jim, Matt Anderson and I again followed the wheat harvest. Toward the end, Jim and I decided to do some sightseeing on the West Coast.

After touring Idaho, Washington, Oregon, Nevada, and California, Jim and I headed home in our Jeepster convertible. Outside of St. Louis, we flipped the car. The windshield and everything above it was smashed. Without means to fix it, we drove home from St. Louis with no windshield or top. The gravel from the road flew in our faces. We were pretty well cooked by the time we got home.

A letter was waiting for me from the draft board that I was to appear the next morning for induction into the

Army as an enlisted man. I called the nearest Naval Officer's Recruiting Office in Cincinnati and they agreed that if I could get to their office before closing time that day, they would swear me into Officer Candidate School in the Navy. I immediately left our house and drove the Jeepster as fast as I could to Cincinnati—this is before interstate highways—and barely got to the recruiting office before it closed.

The Officer Recruiters were visibly shocked by my appearance. I was sunburned and the black gravel was ingrained in my face and neck. The recruiters were trying to think of some gracious way to get rid of me.

They asked the doctors to give me a physical. They moved me from room to room for various examinations. I was undressed, waiting for the next doctor, when I crossed my legs and noticed there was a visible resin on the bottom of my feet. I saw an outline of my flat feet, which is a disqualifier for the Navy. I drew a perfect arch on my left foot and was just changing feet to do the same to my right foot when the doctor came into the exam room. He said, "Raise your left foot." He complimented me on a good arch. He then asked me to raise my other foot, which I did. He exclaimed, "Good heavens, I have never seen someone with only one arched foot." He didn't realize that if he had waited two minutes longer to enter the room, I would have had two perfectly arched feet.

Probably due to it being Friday afternoon and their need to get home for the weekend, they passed me, swore me into the Navy, and wrote official orders for me to continue to my home on a non-paid status until further orders.

Two months later, on January 3, 1953, I entered Naval Officer Candidate School at Newport, Rhode Island, and four months later was commissioned Ensign U.S. Naval Reserve. I was then assigned to the USS Holder, a 2,200-ton destroyer based in Norfolk and attached to the Destroyer Force, U.S. Atlantic Fleet. I served three years aboard this vessel.

For the first year, I was in the Operations Department serving in a wide range of responsibilities including Communication Officer, Crypto-security Officer, Postal Officer, and Electronics Officer. I had undergone a National Agency Security check and held a security clearance to handle classified matter up to and including Top Secret.

In March 1954, I attended an intense seven-week course in Military Law at U.S. Naval School of Justice at Newport, Rhode Island. I was reassigned to legal officer on the Holder. A year later, I completed a 10-week course at the Naval Officer's Damage Control School at Philadelphia, PA, with five weeks study in Damage Control and Fire-fighting and five weeks in Atomic, Biological and Chemical Defense. The USS Holder spent a considerable amount of time in foreign ports, allowing me to visit a total of 22 countries and four continents.

While in the Mediterranean Sea, we made some memorable stops in Algeria, Turkey, and Greece. When we arrived in the Port of Piraeus, I met an American professor of Archeology, who helped me find the Greek relatives of my high school friend, John Collis. The professor located some of John's cousins and they had a nice reception for me with baklava and ouzo, a drink so strong that to this day I avoid any anise-flavored drinks. His cousins generously showed me around their city and then took me back to the ship.

Next we went to Salonica, where we met the military

plane that was carrying our mail. I had radio communications with the pilot and the visibility was so bad he refused to land. I finally found a clearing so the plane could land and we could get long-awaited letters. When we arrived in Izmir, Turkey, I was invited to a Thanksgiving dinner at the home of a military assignee and his wife. I remember I was offered a drink called raki. After one sip, I knew it was anise-based and not for me.

Shortly before I left the Navy, I wrote this about myself on my first resume: "It is obvious that I am not a specialist in any field but I feel that I am young enough, ambitious enough and of sufficient intelligence to succeed in any field of endeavor that presents the challenge and opportunity in which I am interested."

CHAPTER THIRTEEN

Early IBM

Within weeks of leaving the Navy, I secured a job with IBM as a salesperson in Norfolk, VA. Upon starting in Norfolk, there was a reshuffle of territories and I was asked to go to Reading, PA. I agreed and was sent to an intense sales training for a few months in Poughkeepsie, NY.

At the end of 1956, I actively became an IBM salesperson with the territory around Reading. I was selling electric typewriters to manufacturing companies, schools, universities, and churches. I was good at it and exceeded 100% quota every year.

It was 1961 when the first IBM Selectric typewriter came out. I sold 35 of them on the first day they were available and that was unheard of. The Selectric was a game changer in the typewriting world.

I was sharing a house with two IBM bachelors, Jim Nitz and Joe Jalbert. We actually had two houses—one in the city of Reading and one in the country—and we threw frequent parties at both.

I met Judy at a party outside of Philadelphia. Her roommate at Rosemont College happened to be named Patty Hickey. It was because of this connection that she remembered me when I invited her to our annual Christmas Party. She couldn't make it but she sent her regrets back to me, remembering my last name.

During the Christmas holidays, Judy was back in Reading with her family and we saw each other at a formal dance but we both were with other dates. It wasn't until Good Friday the following April that we saw each other again.

Judy loves to tell this story and here is her version:

"My mom, dad and I went to Sacred Heart Church for the Good Friday service. My dad said, 'Let's go have a drink at the club.' Paul and his roommate, Joe, were there. Paul came over to talk to us and he asked me out. Joe was looking for a date and I suggested my sister, Peggi. So they came to our house that night at seven. Dad and I were home but Peggi and Mom had driven to New Jersey for a bridal shower for one of Peggi's college friends. They were supposed to be back in time for the date but they were running very late.

"So I was there at our house with Paul, Joe and my father. I asked them what they wanted to drink and Paul said a bourbon and water and Joe asked for a scotch and water. I guess I was nervous and got the order mixed up. I gave Joe a glass of water and water and Paul got a glass of bourbon and scotch. Paul took a sip and smiled. He said, 'That is my kind of woman!'

"Peggi finally made it home and the double date began. We stayed out very late and the doors were locked when we got back home. We had to go around the back and were about to climb in a window when my mom unlocked the door. That was the very beginning."

CHAPTER FOURTEEN

Meeting Judy

Judy went back to Rosemont College for the end of her senior year and then graduated. She had a summer job at a playground and I would come by to see her. She dated a few other people that summer but by the fall we were going out more and more. Judy was teaching 6th graders in Shillington at a Catholic school and living at home with her parents and four younger brothers. I bought a furnished house during this time.

Before Valentine's Day, I proposed to Judy and she said yes. The previous week, I had called Judy's dad to get his permission to ask for Judy's hand in marriage. He said, "I am too busy now to meet with you but I know why you are calling and it's OK with me."

Judy's dad was a fun-loving Irish guy who worked very hard at his business. Judy's mother was kind and motherly—she had six children. Her German ancestors arrived in the United States in 1749 and later settled in Bally, PA, where we have visited the church and graveyard where they are buried.

We got married that summer on June 24, 1961. We spent our honeymoon sailing in the Chesapeake. We had Karen a year later and then Mike. My two Reading roommates also married people we knew—Joe married Ann Keltz and Jim married Peggi Cauldren, a childhood friend of Judy's who also spent their summers in Stone Harbor, New Jersey.

CHAPTER FIFTEEN

Product Planning in Lexington

In 1964, we moved with IBM to Lexington, Kentucky, and I worked as a product planner. I was the first person at IBM to be hired with the full-time mission to get us into the copier business. I became a senior product planner for the copy machine, which was considered highly secret at the time.

I enjoyed my sales job, got numerous sales awards and was eligible for (and won) the 100% Club. They created a more elite level of sales achievement called The Golden Circle. As a qualifier, I was able to take Judy with me to the extravaganza in Palm Beach, Florida. From there, Judy and I went back to our honeymoon spot and rented the same style boat and cruised inland to Key West and came back on the ocean side.

My years in product planning were always challenging and used every skill I had developed in sales. We had three more children in Lexington—John, Lisa and Julie.

CHAPTER SIXTEEN

Civil Rights Involvement

In the last half of the 1960s, Judy and I were very in
volved in the civil rights movement in Kentucky. In
1966, we were friends with two young priests who were
involved with the Church Community Services (CCS).
This was an interfaith initiative by concerned members
of the Catholic and Protestant faith communities. They
asked if I would be the representative for our parish and
I agreed. I started working with CCS and was eventually
asked to serve as chairman of the board.

The group had several missions but the main one
was community organizing in minority neighborhoods
and promotion of civil rights. (This is what President
Obama did when he got out of college.) We worked with

ministers in Pralltown, a ghetto near the University of Kentucky. The aim was to get to know each other and find out what these communities needed to succeed. City services in the Black communities were abysmal but there was little the residents could do collectively to effect change. Twenty-one churches would meet once a month for a potluck. Sometimes we'd have them in Pralltown and other times we'd meet at other churches but we always rotated locations. Only a few people from our church participated but we recruited a number of our friends to become involved.

William "Billy" Bingham was an energetic and dynamic young African-American man who worked at the University of Kentucky in some capacity and lived in Pralltown. He became actively involved with CCS. (Years later, he was featured in an educational video about Pralltown and its history with the civil rights movement.)

When I was a member of the Kentucky Governor's Commission on Hard-Core Unemployment, I asked Billy to attend the meetings. This commission was charged with identifying causes of unemployment and recommending changes. At an initial meeting, a major

Fortune 500 company representative said his company had attempted to increase minority employment by posting notices for jobs for apprentice draftsmen in a minority community in Louisville but did not get any responses.

Billy told the commission, "If you came into my neighborhood and put up posters offering jobs for apprentice draftsmen, people I know would think, 'I have never met a draftsman and do not know what they do so I am not qualified'—but if you posted a job for someone who can draw, you would get a lot of applicants."

In 1968, the Lexington schools were integrated for the first time. We invited children from our nearby high school and kids from Pralltown to meet at our house to get to know each other. In this way, we were hoping to foster friendships. (This is where the potlucks and other planned get-togethers were most helpful.) The CCS brought volunteers in from out of state during the summers to help. We opened up our home to these volunteers and some came and stayed with us for a night or two.

Pralltown didn't have any playgrounds. There an empty lot where the kids would play. Someone had left an old bedspring and the children would use it as a trampoline. We'd drop off our kids there to play while we were working in the community.

When Martin Luther King was assassinated, another IBM planner and I marched into the office of the top IBM executive in Lexington and said, "You need to do something. IBM must position itself in a positive light." We did not get the reaction we had hoped for.

My nephew Roger Hickey was involved in risky things back then such as voter registration in Mississippi and Virginia. He had no fear of anything. On occasion, he would come through and stay with us. We'd talk about current events. Aunt Bridgie and I accepted Roger during those years. Aunt Bridgie had a strong social conscience and supported what Roger was doing. Dad and Mother were also supportive of social justice causes.

There were numerous instances where civil rights involvement resulted in not so subtle rejection by acquaintances, and even danger at times. What we remember most was the personal fulfillment we felt from contributing in a support role. It put the spotlight on those who could realize their own strength and potential, if improved conditions and different priorities were instituted. Our five young children also gained from this experience by watching us point out the danger of viewing others through the lens of the endemic prejudice of the time.

CHAPTER SEVENTEEN

Ku Klux Klan

I remember when I was young, my Uncle Jimmy King was walking up the road and one of the neighbors, walking the opposite direction and deep in thought, looked up and said, "Good morning, Mr. Catholic." Uncle Jimmy tipped his hat and calmly replied, "Well, good morning Mr. Ku Klux."

There were so few Catholics, Jews and African Americans in our area when I was little that we were all fair game. Other children would call us 'Cat Lickers' instead of Catholics. When I was about eight we saw the KKK on a hill across the road from our house, far enough away that a shotgun couldn't reach them. It was nighttime and they went through their pagan exercises and then burned the cross. We could see it burning from our front porch and knew it was aimed at us. I wasn't scared because everyone was respectful of my dad; he had a presence in the community. But I do remember seeing that cross burning and understanding it was meant to intimidate us.

CHAPTER EIGHTEEN

590 Madison Avenue, New York City

IBM copier development was progressing and I was promoted to Market Research and Forecasting Manager. This required a move closer to the divisional headquarters in Manhattan. So we bought a house in Smoke Rise, New Jersey, an upscale community near Kinnelon. I commuted into New York City.

Before we moved, we had bought a turtle in Lexington and Karen wanted to bring it with her to New Jersey. So we put it in a bowl and Karen was going to take the turtle with her on the plane. (Judy had to fly by herself with the five young kids because I was already in New York working.) Right before they got on the flight, Karen realized she had left the turtle in an airport phone booth. Florence was at the airport with Judy and she ran back to the phone booth but the turtle was gone. Karen cried and was not happy about losing her beloved pet.

Judy said that during the flights to Cincinnati and then onto New Jersey that all five kids were excellent. (By the way, Judy is the most optimistic person I have ever met.) She said all of the kids were very curious and were just in awe looking out the windows at the sky.

I worked insane hours during my time in New York. Since I worked so much, Judy would pack up the kids every Friday afternoon and drive into the city to meet me. IBM had a small parking lot for senior executives at the corner of 57th and Madison Avenue and the attendant let her park there after 5:00. We did a lot of exploring with the kids. We took the Staten Island Ferry, went up the elevators in the tallest skyscrapers, and visited Central Park.

I remember one time we lost John in the Central Park Zoo. He was about four and he was squatting down looking at the monkeys—a lot of people were around—and we didn't see him and walked away. When we realized he was missing, we frantically searched around the zoo and couldn't find him. We returned to the monkey cage. There he was, still mesmerized by the animals.

We also lost Mike around that time period when we were at a large pond in New Jersey. We realized Mike was not with the other kids and we couldn't find him. Everyone at the pond helped us by forming a human chain and looking in their assigned spot in the water. In the end, Mike had gone back to the car. He came back to all of the commotion and we were relieved to see that he was fine. He was probably about five.

Meanwhile, it was an exciting time at work. As manager of market research and forecasting, I would regularly present progress reports to division presidents and other top executives. I stepped on a few toes back then but I had my feet stomped on as well.

After 14 months of tirelessly working at 590 Madison Avenue, the new product that I had been working on all of these years was finally announced: The IBM Copy Machine, which could produce letter or legal size copies from a roll of plain paper at a rate of 600-per-hour. It cost $19,200.

At the time, Xerox dominated the $1.5 billion-a-year

office copier business. They owned about 70 percent of the market share because they had the only plain paper copier. As I mentioned earlier, I was the first person at IBM whose full-time responsibility was to get us into this market, starting back when I was in Reading. I was proud of our ambitious accomplishment.

CHAPTER NINETEEN

Welcome to Austin, Texas

I was offered a job at a fairly new IBM lab site in Austin as the product planning manager for another future product line, which later became the Operating System 6. We decided to relocate to Texas. We moved into the Holiday Inn on I-35 for two weeks while we went house hunting. I had to work every day so Judy and the five kids spent their days with the real estate agent, looking at houses. We found our home at 7708 Shadyrock and moved in on July 22, 1970, fifty years ago.

Judy remembers that someone from the landscape company was to meet us at the Holiday Inn to discuss the yard. He asked the lobby attendant if the Hickey family was at the hotel and the clerk said, "Yes, they are and we'll be glad when they leave!"

The kids would run up and down the hallways and pound on the Coke machines, trying to get extra change to come out. With our five kids ranging in age from 2 to 8, there was never a dull moment during these next several years.

CHAPTER TWENTY

Raising Children in Northwest Hills

Northwest Hills was a new neighborhood in what was considered the outskirts of Austin. It was a bit of a melting pot, with an interesting mix of University of Texas professors, including some international families, small business owners, as well as out-of-state transplants like us, who had just moved to Austin to work at the IBM plant. Some of us had a few things to learn about Texas.

Shortly after we moved in, we invited a German couple for dinner. Everything went well and we enjoyed our evening. When they were ready to leave, we walked them to the front door. "All of a sudden, Paul went crazy," Judy remembers. "He ran to the kitchen and grabbed a broom and darted out to the front yard. He was stabbing the broom into the sidewalk and screaming profanities. Our guests were watching in horror. They ran to their car and never returned." There was an armadillo digging up our newly planted flowers and I was not going to let that thing ruin our new landscaping. Armadillos are nasty animals.

Karen and Mike started at the new neighborhood school, Doss Elementary. Incidentally, it was recently razed and rebuilt and our grandson Scott, will be going there this year. My physician lived across the street and over the years he did several house calls, much to my appreciation.

St. Theresa's Catholic Church had just finished construction at the northern end of the neighborhood and we became very involved there. Westover Hills Club offered swimming and tennis lessons to the kids and social opportunities for the adults. (One year, Judy was a club tennis champion.)

There was still plenty of open space in the neighborhood for the kids to ride their bikes and explore. Nearby were bat caves and the boys would spend hours climbing around in them. The kids were usually off on their own during the days but would always be home for dinner.

We made so many great friends, primarily through IBM, St. Theresa's, and Westover Hills Club. We still see many of them today. IBM used to have parties and picnics, as a way for families to get to know each other outside of work. We met George and Janie Murray through IBM. They also lived nearby and introduced us to their good friends, Elspeth and John Rhodes, who were from England. John worked as a scientist.

Our friendship with Mike and Vivian Hillier started in 1974 when Mike worked for me at IBM. They were British but had taken a two-year assignment in Austin. They loved it so much they ended up staying a third year. We visited them several times in England and France over the years and they have returned to see us in Austin.

Westover Hills Club was a hangout spot for Northwest Hills families on the weekends. I'll never forget the day all of the kids were in the pool and it started to storm. Everyone was told to take cover under the open basketball court that had a metal roof but no walls. The rain came in through the sides so the concrete floor was slick as ice. One of the kids had the great idea to throw themselves on the court and slide across it. The children took turns running as fast as they could and then belly flopping on the court, seeing who could go the farthest.

Never one to pass up fun, I decided to give it a try and join them. I didn't consider the difference in shape and weight between the young children and myself. I ran with all of my might and did a swan dive, landing flat on my stomach, expelling all the air from my lungs. Instead of sliding on the cement floor like I had imagined, I didn't move at all. All the kids thought it was hilarious and jumped on my back. I had an unknown quantity of children on me and I couldn't speak. I found out a few days later when I finally went to the doctor that I had broken two ribs, in addition to my bruises.

CHAPTER TWENTY-ONE

St. Theresa's Catholic Church

We were members of St. Theresa's on Small Drive from when they first opened their doors in 1971. We met some of our closest friends at this time, including Jerry and Jean Olson, who also belonged to the Westover Hills Club. We were very active in Marriage Encounter, where we met John and Pat O'Neil. The Dunlaps and Hutchesons joined the church later and became part of our social circle. All these years later, we still see a lot of them, as well as their kids or even their grandkids, at different get-togethers. Up until recently, we met monthly for twenty years with our four-couple dinner club.

I have always been conscientious that I belong to a family that can trace its Catholic roots to our forefathers, who for more than 700 years have had an unbroken streak of being Catholics. Judy and I both grew up in Catholic homes and attended Catholic schools. It was important to me to continue this tradition, even if there were points in time when I didn't agree with the Church teachings. I might oppose something they teach this century but that is immaterial to the essence of what has been taught over the centuries.

Judy and I taught religious education, were Eucharistic ministers, and were involved in fundraisers of all sorts for many years. Judy was active with Lifeline that provided assistance to pregnant girls including bilingual counselors, clothing drives, and diaper distributions.

We made friends in the Hispanic community when we would attend Spanish mass at other churches. It was important to us to show our children the value of having friends from diverse ethnic backgrounds. As a result, I think our children are open-minded.

CHAPTER TWENTY-TWO

Hickey Hotel

Our Shadyrock home was sometimes nicknamed The Hickey Hotel. There was always someone staying with us. The Irish would say, "The latchkey was always out." We had a constant stream of family and friends.

Judy's sister, Peggi Purcell, lived with us for a year. She stayed in Austin and now lives about ten miles from us. My nephew John Wickens and his friend, Tim, stayed with us for a few weeks and John's sister, Rita, came for an extended stay. My sisters Florence and Christine would visit from Kentucky and Dot and Larry would drive down from Montana periodically. Judy's siblings from the East Coast would come stay with us. Judy's mother lived with us during her final year.

In addition, the kids' friends would always be at our house. The philosophy seemed to be the more the merrier. I remember when one of John's friends was leaving our house one day and his parents were enthusiastically thanking me. I didn't know why they seemed so appreciative until Judy told me later that he had been staying with us for two weeks while his parents were in Colorado. I had no idea that his stay had been continuous.

Charles Hillier, the son of our friends from England, came to stay with us while he was attending a tennis academy and then remained at our house for almost a year. He was at least 6'5" and was a fun guy to have around. His sister also stayed with us one summer when the girls were in high school and again when she was traveling around the world.

When the kids were young, we went to the beach in Port Aransas and met some hippies, who had just come down from New Jersey. Since we had also moved to Texas from New Jersey, we struck up a conversation with them. Being friendly, we invited them to stop by, if they were ever in Austin. Next thing we knew, they came to Shadyrock, pitched their tent in our backyard, and stayed for a few nights.

We had an exchange student from Guanajuato, Mexico. Julie spent half the summer with her family and then she stayed with us the rest of the summer. Our young nephew, Tom Purcell, moved to Austin after college and spent a few years on and off at our house. He is still in the Austin area and we always enjoy his visits.

The Rileys, our life-long friends who we first met in Reading, had moved with IBM to Houston and we saw each other a lot. We traveled with them on many family vacations—to Colorado, Montana, Bermuda, Jamaica, and an unforgettable trip to Mexico when we all got sick. Judy and Mary Lou were pregnant with Karen and Jeff at the same time in Reading, so our bond with them goes way back. Our children call them Aunt Mary Lou and Uncle Herb. They would visit us in Austin and we would spend a lot of summer weekends with them, all crammed in their A-frame house on Lake LBJ.

CHAPTER TWENTY-THREE

Potpourri of Advanced Technology

The initial reason I relocated to Austin was because I was working on a new concept and line of products called Operating System 6 (OS/6), dubbed the "Rio" project. It included a stand-alone word processor with computer input and output. It featured a keyboard, display, and the first letter-quality ink jet printer. Documents were stored on floppy disks and magnetic stripe cards. The OS/6 could be used by large organizations to allow mail merge, to use high quality printing with many formatting options, and to print directly on envelopes, among other features.

Our team implemented proportional spacing as an option on all of our products. This is a formatting technique where certain letters take up more space than others. We also worked on the ability to print in multiple columns. These were great leaps forward, such as going from pencil to typing.

The OS/6 had communication and spreadsheet capabilities. (Mike Hillier told people for years that I developed the first spreadsheet.) At the time, it was mind-boggling how far ahead IBM was with this product line. It was the incipient stages of databases and the easy manipulating of data. Sadly, it didn't meet its full potential because it was a high-price, low-volume product. But it was the beginning.

I was part of a group that created a dual purpose for the IBM Selectric typewriter so it could serve as a teaching tool for keypunch machines by changing out the typing element or the "silver golf ball head." Schools could justify buying the product because key punch training had not been taught in schools previously and this allowed them to teach typing and keypunch with the same device. It costs IBM virtually nothing to add keypunch training and it proved to be very profitable.

Since I had started at IBM, I watched the company

enter the typewriter, copier, printer, and word processing markets. Now IBM was moving toward microprocessors and computers. Later in my career, when I was working with The Open Group, I put together IBM executives in the U.S. with Lenovo management in China. This collaboration resulted in Lenovo buying the whole laptop product line from IBM. It was a very rarified world I was in for a while and I loved it.

CHAPTER TWENTY-FOUR

Who's Driving What?

Since our teenage children were so close in age, they all had drivers licenses at the same time. Unlike many families that gave a car to each child, we took the fleet approach. Basically, the first person to get into the car could drive it for the day. Of course, the early bird always picked the best one.

Judy and I had our cars—usually a station wagon and a sedan—but the ever-changing assortment of unique, interesting and cheap vehicles was up for grabs. Over the years, we had a Datsun, Mazda, Mercedes, Volkswagen, a couple of beat-up work trucks, and numerous others.

What we later realized was that none of our kids had a sense of pride of ownership. If they ran out of gas, they would call me. If they got in a scrape, they'd call me. I am sure none of them was changing the oil. In short, our kids drove the cars into the ground. Luckily, we discovered an excellent resource—a young man who was starting a body shop operation. He did good work and was very inexpensive since he was just beginning. We certainly kept him busy. At times, we owned seven cars, all parked around our house.

I remember we had just had major bodywork done on one side of our Datsun 280Z. The kids called it the "Z Car" and loved to drive it. Later that same day, one of the children scratched the other side of the car against something. We took it back to the repairman. He looked at me funny but didn't say anything too derogatory. After picking up the car the following day, another one of the kids was driving in the neighborhood during a rare ice storm, lost control and wrecked it a third time. When I took it back to our mechanic, he looked at me astounded and asked, "Mr. Hickey, what are you doing to this car?" This is when I had the revelation that the fleet concept was no good. The kids would have their own cars going forward and they would have to maintain it themselves.

One of our worst purchases we ever made was a Peugeot, a French diesel sedan. Since there were very few of these cars in Central Texas, there was no dealer to help with repairs. Again, we found a shade tree mechanic that was in love with Peugeots. He was Irish but spent much of his life in France so he had a very strong accent. He barely spoke English, except to curse.

He lived a few hours away in Wimberley so when he would come work on our car, he would stay the night with us. He would spend the whole time in our garage, working on the car. If anyone criticized the car, he would go ballistic. No one could say anything negative about the Peugeot. He clearly had something wrong with him because two out of every three words out of his mouth were loud curse words so bad I couldn't print them.

The neighbors must have thought we had a used car lot with a crazy person working for us. They were too polite—or too scared—to ever complain to us.

Karen took one of the Volkswagens to college. One of the more bizarre collisions was when she ran into a Lubbock detective vehicle. I took it to another shade tree mechanic who worked in a junkyard and he basically took a large rock and pounded on the fender to try to straighten it back in place. Bringing it home after the repair job did not make Karen very happy because there wasn't much improvement. I admit it was not the most prestigious vehicle for her to drive.

About this time, John had a summer job working in construction. He was making good money and told us he didn't need to go to college because he liked this work. On a particularly hot August afternoon, after John had been framing a three-story office building, he came home and told me he changed his mind about college. I asked him why and he said he looked around the job site and noticed that people his age were making the same amount of money as people my age. "Time alone didn't get you ahead," he said. "I want to get into a profession that when I am your age I am making more money than I did at my age."

CHAPTER TWENTY-FIVE

The Shark

During a business conference in Miami, I went deep-sea fishing with several co-workers and I caught a hammerhead shark. I decided it was a keeper so I had it stuffed and mounted and shipped to our home. I hung this ten-foot shark over our fireplace for several years.

George Murray was over for dinner and was telling us about a restaurant that he had just bought in Georgetown. He thought it would be a nice feature to have the shark as wall decor in his restaurant and asked if I would consider selling it. I said, "How much?" He made an acceptable offer and I said, "Sold!" Judy and Janie weren't listening to the conversation and were surprised when George and I jumped up from the dinner table and took the shark off the wall. We somehow got it into his car. By that time, I was ready to see the shark go.

The shark was the topic of many conversations at our house. One of our children's friends thought it was caught in nearby Lake Travis. I had fun playing along with that joke.

CHAPTER TWENTY-SIX

Desegregation

In 1980, Austin Independent School District implemented a cross-town busing program to equalize the racial balance of schools. The intention was for certain high schools to be more reflective of the population of Austin at the time. Our neighborhood was split down the middle as far as the boundary of who would go to which high school. As a result, Mike, John, Lisa, and Julie had to go to A.S. Johnston High School about 20 miles away in East Austin. Karen had already graduated from Anderson High School, less than a mile from our house.

We were interested in getting to know the administration at Johnston High School so we became officers of the PTA. It gave us a chance to get to know the school, the teachers and the other students.

We were one of the few families in Northwest Hills that were in favor of the busing. We had been involved in the civil rights movement, trying to facilitate change, so we saw the merit to this program, mainly to have our children go to school with a more diverse student body.

Our children got to know students from every part of town. For our family, it was a wonderful experience. Judy and I went to all of the sporting events. Mike played baseball, John was on the golf team, and Lisa and Julie were cheerleaders.

CHAPTER TWENTY-SEVEN

Real Estate and Family Travel

We got interested in real estate, which became a hobby that kept us busy for years. We were sitting at a baseball game watching the boys play and I saw an ad for a duplex. I decided we would go look at it, right then and there. Judy and I drove over to see it and bought it. We made it back in time for the end of the baseball game. This was the beginning of a consuming interest for both of us. Judy managed a large number of rental properties, including our own, and those of other IBM investors. I worked during the evenings and on weekends.

Our largest investment was a commercial building purchased at 2nd and Trinity, adjacent to the current convention center. At the time, not much was in the area.

On Sunday mornings, we would all go to 9:00 a.m. Mass, come home and change into work clothes. We all piled into the station wagon, packed with the lawn mower and cleaning and painting supplies. We would work on our rental properties.

My inclination was that our children were virtually free labor. Judy, on the other hand, argued they should get the same amount of pay that we would pay someone else. As soon as we put this into effect, the kids who dragged their feet before suddenly became workaholics. In addition to our children, they would recruit their friends who needed money. We got to know a lot of the more ambitious young people in Northwest Hills.

Judy pointed out it was not all work and no play. We had a ski boat on Lake Travis and spent our Sundays on the lake. I probably taught more neighborhood kids how to ski than anyone else. On the way home, we would stop and get nickel pizza slices.

We bought a travel trailer and explored a number of Texas State Parks. We fell in love with Port Aransas and kept up an annual trip there for almost thirty years. IBM gave me five weeks of summer vacation and major holidays off so we had the luxury of planning extended trips.

One of our longest drives in the trailer was to Kentucky, where I had a business meeting, and then onto Montana to see relatives and back to Texas via Yellowstone. We had the five kids, our dog Missy, and my sister Florence on the trip with us. We also drove to the New York harbor to see the Tall Ships and to Philadelphia in 1976 to see the Liberty Bell.

I remember on one of our longer trips, we stopped at Stuckey's to get gas and snacks. Getting the children back in the car was always a major ordeal. It was like herding cats. If they wouldn't get in, I would swat them on the rear. That time, the last kid was delaying getting in the car so I swatted him. I looked up and saw a tall menacing man glaring at me. I realized the boy I had just spanked was not my own. His dad and I were both frozen with surprise. I recovered faster, jumped in the car, and drove out of the parking lot as fast as possible.

When the kids were teenagers, Judy's brothers, Dan and Jim Purcell, asked if we wanted to go snow skiing with them. They were excellent skiers. Jim was an instructor, and they agreed to teach our children how to ski. They had their work cut out for them but eventually all of our children could tackle black diamond runs. Judy remembers her brothers would make the kids put their hat between their knees at the top of the slope and not be able to put it back on their head until they got to the bottom. This taught them to ski with their knees together.

Every year our Christmas gift to the kids was a ski trip to Colorado. We stayed at most of the minor and major ski resorts over the years, including Winter Park, Aspen, and Vail. Judy's mother would come with us and sit in the lodge with our belongings and save a table for our lunch spot. When Julie lived in Jackson Hole we skied there several times, as well as a few trips to New Mexico and Utah.

Judy and I had opposite ski styles. We would take the lift up together. At the top of the slope, Judy would point her skis to the side and slowly and carefully zigzag her way down. She almost never fell. I, on the other hand, would point my skis straight down the mountain and go at breakneck speed. I would wipe out constantly. Because of Judy's careful speed and my not-so-infrequent falls, the two of us would usually end up at the bottom of the slope at about the same time and get back on the lift together for another run. Looking back, this was an ideal family trip for all of us during the kids' high school and college years.

CHAPTER TWENTY-EIGHT

Montana Connection

Over the years, our family has enjoyed many vacations to visit our relatives in Montana in and around Winifred. The Wickens were cattle ranchers, wheat farmers and road builders. Many of the interstate highways in the state were built by their equipment and labor. The next generation now raises cattle and run a hunting outfitting operation. The Hickey relatives in Winifred own and operate many businesses in town, including the bar, an upscale steakhouse restaurant, and a hotel.

For our 50th wedding anniversary, the entire family spent a week in Montana, staying in the family hunting lodges. The grandchildren rode horses, looked for dinosaur bones, shot guns, and swam in the nearby Judith River. Together, the Hickey and Wickens relatives number over 100 people.

CHAPTER TWENTY-NINE

South America

My first experience in South America was when Herb Riley and I went to Brazil to check on a diamond mine that he had invested in. It turned out to be quite a two-week adventure. We started in Rio de Janeiro before we headed out to Manaus, where we got into a dugout canoe to go river fishing on the Amazon. We flew to Mato Grosso near the rainforest—this was close to where the diamond mine was located. The area dates back to the 18th century gold rush and is considered the wild west. Everyone we encountered was armed.

When we finally found the mine, Herb saw that his partners had not spent the money on the mine development but instead had built a very nice house next to the mine. Herb was incensed and was chewing out the workers. I was standing a distance away from Herb near a few of the other workers. A bird flew low over our heads. At the same time, they all pulled out their guns and shot the bird in flight. On impact, the bird disintegrated in front of my eyes; all I saw were feathers. I got real quiet about then.

During the trip, I bought diamonds and semi-precious stones—specifically tourmalines—directly from the source. Since I had to return to Texas and the diamonds still needed to be cut, Herb's Brazilian partner later hand delivered the cut stones to me in Austin.

Later when I worked The Open Group, I was responsible for Central and South America, giving me business reasons to travel to Brazil on several occasions.

Our daughter Lisa volunteered for the Peace Corps in Ecuador for two years. I had a business trip to Chile and extended my time to visit her. She lived in Nambacola, a small village in the Andean highlands. I flew into Quito and she met me at the airport. We were supposed to fly down to her town but there was a domestic airline strike and no one knew how many days or weeks it would last. So Lisa and I flagged down a taxi in front of our hotel and asked the driver if he could take us to and from Nambacola, a two-day drive each way. Without hesitating, he agreed. He quickly drove home to pack a suitcase and came back to pick us up. We spent the next week traveling through Ecuador in our rented taxi with our new best friend, the driver.

I then flew to Santiago, Chile, for business and got to see one of my old friends from Reading, PA. He was now a successful Chilean businessman who owned one of the largest pencil manufacturing companies in South America. He lived in a beautiful home that was located halfway between the beach and the mountains. He told me he could swim in the ocean in the morning and then snow ski in the afternoon.

Judy and I went back to Ecuador the following year to see Lisa again. This time, we traveled north of Quito. We have a picture of us standing on the equator—one foot in the northern hemisphere and one in the southern hemisphere. We stopped at the nearby Otavalo Market that has one of the largest indigenous markets in Latin America. I remember seeing a small old Indian woman carrying a heavy load of straw on her head, knitting a sweater and running down the hill toward her booth. I had to buy a straw hat from her.

CHAPTER THIRTY

Yellowstone

After 35 years, I formally retired from IBM in 1991. The first summer after retirement, Judy and I went to visit Julie, who was living in Jackson, Wyoming. We had a nice time exploring the area.

One day we drove into Yellowstone and went into the gift shop. We noticed the employees seemed to be about our age and they were having a lot of fun. We struck up conversations with several of them, many of whom were retired and working in the park for the season.

I asked one man how we could get a job there. He said it was perfect timing because the college students only want to work in the summer and they would be leaving soon, opening up many positions. Judy filled out an application form and we didn't think about it again.

When we returned to Austin at the end of July, we received a letter from Yellowstone National Park that we could report to work in three days. So we got in the car and drove up to Wyoming to start our new "post retirement" job.

We lived on the second floor of the store, which had married-couples rooms and dormitory-style bathrooms. On our first day of work, Judy was assigned to a wonderful job in the gift department and I was to work in men's apparel. On day one, I had to unload a large trailer truck of merchandise outside in the heat. It was extremely strenuous labor and I desperately wanted to leave. Meanwhile, Judy was enjoying talking to tourists in the air-conditioned store.

I stuck it out and found out later that they put all new employees through this test of endurance. Luckily, I never had to do it again. The days went by and we loved driving around the park and seeing the animals at their finest. One of the highlights was seeing a grizzly bear eating the carcass of a dead buffalo.

We had the weekends off and we would go into Jackson to spend time with Julie. Once we met Dot and Larry in Big Sky, Montana, and spent two nights at a hotel on the top of mountain. The last day, Dot was driving us down the steep winding road from Big Sky. She was driving like a racecar driver and she scared Judy to death. We finished out the six weeks of our work assignment in Yellowstone and drove back to Austin.

Judy and I had discovered Continental Airlines Freedom Passports for people 62 or older. It allowed seniors to travel anywhere Continental flew for a deeply discounted yearly flat fee and we each bought one for a few years in a row. For a retirement gift, my former colleague gave us a timeshare for two weeks in St. Croix that we booked during this time.

Since all of our children were living in what we considered desirable or resort locations, and we had free time, we made it a point to visit them. We saw Karen in Sundance, Utah and Philadelphia; Mike in San Antonio; John in Escondido, California on the oceanfront; Lisa in Manhattan on Central Park West; and Julie in Jackson Hole.

CHAPTER THIRTY-ONE

Lateral Solutions, Inc.

At this point, I had the opportunity to become a contractor for IBM. I formed a corporation and set up an office on Jollyville Road, near 183.

I named my company Lateral Solutions based on an article I read about one of the world's tallest skyscrapers. It was built and rented out before the owner realized the elevators were inadequate. There was a mad rush in the morning of people waiting to get on the elevator and it led to complaining and frustration.

The builder hired several consultants, who proposed a variety of expensive ideas such as rebuilding the elevator to make it bigger or adding another elevator. One consultant simply suggested adding mirrors in the lobby right in front of the elevator. They tried this approach and found there was the same amount of people waiting for the elevator in the morning but the workers weren't complaining anymore. Instead, they were occupied looking at themselves in the mirror. The article called this a lateral solution. I liked that thought process of a non-standard but effective fix to a difficult problem.

Lateral Solutions provided contractors—usually engineers and IT architects—to the department in IBM that did global consulting. The advantage of my company was that all of my employment agreements stated they could join IBM as permanent employees, if offered. This made my company unique.

One contract that I was providing resource for was The Open Group. After a short time of contracting with them, they asked if I would be interested in a full-time job with The Open Group in Asia. They needed to start another office there; they had just hired someone to open one in Japan. I accepted the position and started to research which Asian country would be best. Meanwhile, Judy was packing up the Shadyrock house so we could rent it out during our new assignment abroad.

CHAPTER THIRTY-TWO

Hong Kong

I chose Hong Kong for the office location. I flew over before Judy so I could get started. I rented an office, formed a corporation, hired a secretary, and took care of the other requirements. In addition to growing membership, my business goal was to expand The Open Group scope to offer highly qualified consultants in Hong Kong, Japan and Australia. During those two years, I took the Asian territory from almost non-existent to a growing concern.

One of the most exciting events we ever experienced was the handover of Hong Kong to China on July 1, 1997, ending 156 years of British colonial rule. It was a multi-day extravaganza and tourists had flown in from around the world to witness it. On the last night of British control before the transfer of sovereignty, England put on a spectacular fireworks display over the Hong Kong Harbor, as the royal yacht, flying the British flag, exited the harbor with the governor and other VIPs onboard. Through a client, Julian Startgardt, we were able to watch everything close up from a downtown office building.

The second night of events was the first day under Chinese rule and they wanted to put on a better show than England. China is known for their elaborate fireworks and we had thought the first night was great but the second night was more than anyone would ever expect. We were watching it from the outside pool deck at the J.W. Marriott. Our daughter Lisa was visiting us at the time and we all agreed it was unlikely we would ever witness a fireworks competition as spectacular as this.

It was surprisingly quiet after the handover and life appeared to continue as normal in Hong Kong. We did notice, however, that all signs with "Royal" were removed. Also, the Chinese military were not visible on the streets, whereas the uniformed British soldiers had been out and about.

The first year we lived on Lantau Island in a beautiful three-bedroom apartment with a rooftop garden that gave us a scenic view of the harbor. No automobiles were allowed on the island; only privately owned golf carts and mini-buses for transportation to the ferry. There was a significant expat community there. My commute was a bus to the pier, a ferry to Hong Kong Island, the underground subway to the area of my office, and a short walk to the building.

The second year we moved into the Grand Hyatt hotel where we remained until returning to the U.S. in 1999. We lived in the lap of luxury, a far different experience than my year in a one-room schoolhouse in Montana. We were able to negotiate a favorable price and the hotel honored it for our entire stay. We were assigned a luxury suite, where the living room had a panoramic view of the harbor and the hills.

We learned that when you are a permanent resident of an upscale hotel, there are a lot of perks. We were given a membership to the private club where we were served breakfast every morning and cocktail hour every afternoon. We became good friends with the head chef, who often provided us special delicacies from the kitchen. We were assigned a hotel ambassador, Ann Gao, whose job was to keep us comfortable all year. She arranged for us to attend special events. We took part in the launch party for Ansett Australia Airlines. During the event, they assigned us the first two frequent flyer numbers in the program—I was #1 and Judy was given #2. Subsequently, we frequently flew on Ansett during my business trips to Australia.

The Hyatt's private driver took us to and from the airport in their Mercedes limousine whenever we flew. The hotel also had an English taxi that could drive us around town. The Open Group let Judy fly with me on all of my trips since the hotel would store our possessions during our trips and not charge us for the nights we were away, making it cheaper for them to buy Judy's plane ticket rather than pay the hotel bill.

We established many close friendships during our time in Asia. We met Chinese and Filipino friends through the Catholic Church, where we attended weekly mass. In fact, Karen and her family came to visit us and her son, Michael, who was an infant, was baptized at the Catholic Church there on Lantau Island.

We had become friends with our Australian Paulist priest and offered him our apartment as a place to stay if any parishioners were ever in need. On Christmas Eve, Father Ginnivan showed up unexpectedly at our front door with a Filipina woman and her two young daughters—a three-year-old and a baby. She had been beaten up by her expat husband. She and her daughters stayed with us for two weeks. While keeping her in hiding, we were able to get volunteer resources to pay for their transportation back to the Philippines. When this was completed, we were shocked to hear she returned to her husband.

Judy volunteered at the orphanage in Hong Kong when I was at work. She and a group of women would take the children out for walks in the city. She said the kids loved to touch everything—the walls, trees, etc. Even though they didn't speak English, Judy said they somehow all communicated with each other and had fun. The walks would culminate in a lunch outing at McDonald's.

On other days, Judy would volunteer inside the orphanage, holding the babies. She loved this but said it was heartbreaking because staff didn't hold them or give them much stimulation. She was told the local families would put their baby in an orphanage because they didn't have enough money at that particular time. They intended to bring the child home at a later date but often that didn't happen.

I got a glimpse into the Hong Kong medical system when I had major back surgery and was hospitalized for two weeks. I was in a private hospital and my room was large and comfortable and the staff was wonderful. That said, it gave me pause when my surgeon introduced himself to me and his name was Dr. Quack. There was quite a difference though between the private and public hospitals. One of our close friends had twins and we visited her in the public hospital. She was sharing a small room with her newborns and another woman with newborn twins.

This friend of ours also had a four-year old daughter, Nicola, who we would occasionally babysit. (The husband was a Kenyan airline pilot and would be gone for work, so we wanted to help out his wife). One day when Nicola was leaving our apartment, she said, "Paul, I love you with all my heart and soul!"

Our friends in Hong Kong were all ages. Even though Judy was about 60 and I was about 70, one of our closest friends was 30-year-old Ann Gao. She introduced us to many of her young friends who were multinational and multilingual. Judy Kim, a 30-something Korean friend, organized monthly Friday night Korean dinner parties. She would email her friends to see if they wanted to meet that week at a Korean restaurant of her choosing. She knew many of the owners so they would reserve a private room just for us. Anywhere between ten to 35 people would join. Judy Kim's parents came a few times and they were about our age. Kelly Werner, our good friend who was one of Julie's college friends at Mary Baldwin College, came with us several times. It was a diverse group and always enjoyable.

Luckily, Judy and I love to travel because we were always on the go. Our Asian destinations were Japan, Taiwan, Macau, Singapore, Korea, Mainland China, Philippines, Australia, Tasmania, India, Thailand, Malaysia, and Indonesia.

One time we inadvertently had a literal around-the-world trip. We had two scheduled meetings—in Boston and Reading, England. Upon arriving in Boston from Hong Kong, we were told the meetings had been canceled. So we re-booked our ticket and flew to London and then back to Hong Kong via India. We circled the globe in about five days.

On any month that we had not traveled, we would take the short trip to Macau on the high-speed hydrofoil to get our passports stamped. Hong Kong required that United States citizens could only stay 30 days without a work permit. Therefore, we needed to travel monthly to another country to update our passport. Macau was established as a Portuguese settlement in 1557 and still had unique colonial architecture. We enjoyed walking around town during occasional daytrips.

Toward the end of our time in Hong Kong, I had planned to relocate the office to Australia. I built a case that we should move the office to Sydney. The CEO agreed, subject to approval by the board of directors. I went to Sydney and formed an office, found a house to rent, and hired an immigration firm to get our secretary to Australia. When this was all done, the board actually declined the request to move the headquarters. Additionally, they felt that my successful consultant business was in direct competition with the board's own consulting businesses; companies including IBM and Hewlett Packard. I was told to shut down the Hong Kong and Sydney offices and return to work in Menlo Park, California. Judy and I moved to California, rented a nice apartment in Silicon Valley right before we celebrated the beginning of the new millennium, which we celebrated in downtown San Francisco.

We stayed in California for fourteen months and then moved back to our house on Shadyrock, when it occurred to me that it didn't matter where in the world I lived because at that point my job involved either travel or communications over the phone or internet. At this time, my son Mike was between jobs and got hired as a consultant for The Open Group. The company liked the job he was doing and asked him to join full time. He is still employed with them.

CHAPTER THIRTY-THREE

The Open Group

Initially, my responsibility remained with the Asia Pacific region. Then through some personnel changes, my duties changed to membership sales in the U.S. and Europe and other revenue-producing activities. Eventually, I was responsible for worldwide revenue, including personal certification fees and training course provider licenses, the most important one being TOGAF®, The Open Group Architecture Framework. I was one of two people responsible for keeping this product growing and it became the leading architecture framework in the world today.

I was also in charge of software licenses, including the UNIX® Operating System, which was the worldwide standard for operating systems in mid-range computers. The Open Group owns the UNIX trademark. The sales team and others worked directly for me during this period of time and we always met our growth goals.

I continued to attend quarterly worldwide conferences, which pleased Judy immensely because she always traveled with me. We went to England, Scotland, Denmark, Ireland, Germany, France, Spain, Portugal, Italy, Amsterdam, Belgium, Hungary, and probably a few more I can't remember.

For the next 15 years, I continued at this job with Judy and I traveling frequently to Europe. It was a wonderful time for us—the international trips, coupled with the stimulating work. When I turned 85, I thought it was about time I should retire. (No one that worked with me had any idea I was in my mid-eighties.) It is interesting to note that the year before I retired, I received the most significant promotion in my entire career. This included responsibilities for Brazil and all of Central and South America.

The Open Group's executive staff arranged a big retirement party for me in Amsterdam and invited members and customers from across the world. Unfortunately, this was a surprise party and no one told me about it. Judy and I had already arranged a Baltic cruise and we could not change our tickets.

They re-scheduled the retirement party to coincide with the following conference in Boston in July. We invited Judy's brother and his wife, Dan and Robin Purcell, who lived nearby. It was a very well done event, on a beautiful evening on the water, and it meant so much to us.

Having worked since I was 12 years old, I had to ease my way into retirement. I continued with The Open Group in a limited capacity, auditing certification trainers. Also, I had maintained my Texas real estate broker's license all of these years, primarily helping friends and family with transactions.

It was last year at age 91 that I would say I truly retired when I released my Texas real estate broker's license and stepped away from all formal activities. Looking back at my career, I can see an intertwining or string of knowledge from each job that then added value to my performance in my subsequent position.

For example, the intensive sales training that I initially received at IBM, along with the next eight years as a salesman, made me more effective at every corporate job I held afterwards. The years I spent in product development of the copy machine helped me in my future position with marketing and forecasting of the word processor. This timeframe became the foundation for my next project, which was a convergence of word processing, data processing and computing. All of my positions at IBM directly impacted my success on a more global scale at The Open Group.

Additionally, my work allowed me to meet people from around the country and the world, many of whom became my good friends. Colleagues have visited us in Austin from as far away as Hong Kong, Australia, England and France. Our door has always been open to welcome those I have worked with and gotten to know on a personal level. All of these relationships have been invaluable.

CHAPTER THIRTY-FOUR

Progeny

For my 80th and Judy's 70th birthdays, our children told us to pick any place in the world that we wanted to go and they would treat us to a first class trip there. This included plane tickets, hotels, guided tours and any other expenses. We decided to go to Argentina and Uruguay. Judy's favorite part of the trip was watching the locals on a Sunday afternoon tango dancing in a park. She laughed when the elderly women kept asking me to tango with them.

For our 57th wedding anniversary, the kids again pitched in and treated us to an Alaskan cruise. We were upgraded to the royal suite that had a large living room, a wide balcony, a stocked bar, and a full-time personal butler. Since Julie was turning fifty, she came with us.

During the time our kids were in college, our real estate holdings went south and we had financial problems. All of the children took it in stride and were willing to cut back, as needed. It was an especially difficult time for Judy and I but the kids helped out and continued with their education.

Judy and I feel like we did something right in raising our children. All five of them are outstanding individuals and have married high-caliber spouses. I can say the same about their offspring: we have 13 grandchildren and they are all unique, academically bright, and just fun to be around. They are athletic and involved in many sports and other activities. We can't imagine anything better than being surrounded by our grandkids. I think of that bible verse about cast your bread upon the waters and get back tenfold.

Karen and Rob settled down in Virginia Beach to raise their four sons—Ian, Michael, Luke and Robert—and they took full advantage of living near the ocean and building their dream home with a boat dock and tennis court. Their kids are well-educated and well-adjusted young men. Their family inherited our travel bug. They have taken many international trips and so far, a few of their sons have done exchange programs in Australia, South Africa, and the Czech Republic.

Mike has followed my professional path with experience in software sales and particularly in following my lead in working for The Open Group. He has been responsible for some worldwide standards, some of which have provided a major improvement for military communications. Mike and his wife, Susan, built a lakefront second home on Lake Marble Falls and have enjoyed many relaxing weekends there with their sons, Paul and Scott. They live nearby and we enjoy seeing them frequently.

John has built an impressive business based in Houston. He started in the watch industry and has expanded into other products and distribution channels. His business requires him to travel to Europe and he has taken his wife, Melinda, and sons, Joel and Matthew, on multiple trips. His sons have become quite familiar with London, Paris, and Geneva. I am proud that both of his sons have achieved Eagle Scout rank.

Lisa and Jim and their daughters, Bridget and Charlotte, live near Lake Travis. Jim has built a good reputation as a builder in that area. Lisa served in the Peace Corps, then obtained her Master's Degree from Columbia University and now works in medical research and writes freelance. After six grandsons, Bridget and Charlotte became our first granddaughters. We have particularly enjoyed attending their sporting events as loyal fans.

When Julie was college age, we were in a financial bind. Julie responded in her usual positive way and she shifted into warp speed to finish her studies in three years rather than the traditional four. She convinced her college advisor to count her summer bartending job at a London pub as a life experience worth college credit. Julie later received a Berkeley-Columbia Executive MBA while she was working full time at Intuit. Julie and her wife, Lori, live in Davis, California, with their three children, Jackson, Lucy and Ellie. They are engaged parents and spend much time at their kids' activities, including soccer and live theater.

We have been fortunate as adults that our children

have wanted to spend a lot of time with us at our home. Our children, and their friends, often stop by to visit. When we were building our house all those years ago, I struck a deal with our builder to add an extended back patio, which was almost as large as the first floor of our house. It was designed for entertainment. When the kids were young it was used for toys and a rolling skating rink. In later years, it became a general meeting place for friends and family. It has gotten lots of use over the years.

Every Thanksgiving, our extended family comes from all over the country to Shadyrock to spend the holiday together. We have our traditions—we go bowling at Dart Bowl, which sadly just closed down; we play tennis and eat barbeque; we have our annual Hickey Family Christmas picture taken; and we stuff ourselves at the Thanksgiving feast. The most special part of this tradition is realizing year after year that everyone in our family really likes each other.

CHAPTER THIRTY-FIVE

Why Hat?

When our first grandson, Ian, was a toddler and learning to speak, his mother, Karen, would point at objects and say table, chair, etc. She pointed at my hat, which I do always wear, and said hat. Ian assumed she was pointing at me and he instantly called me "Hat" from then on. Thereafter, all of the grandchildren and their friends, and almost everyone else I know, now call me "Hat."

CHAPTER THIRTY-SIX

Love of My Life

Looking back, I consider it great luck to have found Judy. We knew we had common interests when I changed our honeymoon at the last minute from a more traditional New Brunswick land tour to a rented cabin cruiser on Chesapeake Bay.

Judy had already bought her clothes for Canada. I was in Annapolis the weekend before with a group of friends from Reading and I met someone who rented yachts. I asked if they had one available for the next week for my honeymoon. I called Judy and told her that we had the opportunity to switch our honeymoon to an unforgettable and unique cruise on a 30-foot Chris Craft cabin cruiser on the Chesapeake. Judy said she thought it was a good idea. Unbeknownst to her, I had already put the deposit down for the rental and was relieved she agreed.

This led to a lifetime of adventure, as time has gone by. Judy has always been up for anything. She is very positive and chooses to see the best side in everything—including me.

I attribute the longevity of our loving relationship to our involvement in Marriage Encounter many years before. This was not marriage counseling but instead was a program that had started in Spain to make good marriages stronger. We attended one of the first United States weekend seminars in New York. When we moved to Texas, we continued with the organization and it helped to strengthen our marriage through the years. I will never forget what someone said to me during one of the meetings: The best thing you can do for your children is to love their mother. I can honestly say that I have truly loved Judy.

CHAPTER THIRTY-SEVEN

Focus on Building Strengths

Everyone has strengths and weaknesses. I saw early in my career that many managers spent time trying to get employees to correct their faults. Everyone knows their weaknesses—their first grade teacher or high school instructor already pointed them out many years before. Highlighting someone's faults is usually a useless exercise and often makes the person feel ashamed. I always choose the opposite philosophy. If you find people's strengths, and assign their responsibilities to align with them, you will see that exponential growth is possible.

I had to apply this same philosophy to myself. I learned a long time ago that I was more of a generalist than a specialist. I have always been comfortable pursuing diverse jobs that provided new and unique challenges. I had to accept this about myself and realize that I would probably not have one specific area of expertise.

It was about 75 years ago that I made a plan to experience as much of life as reasonably possible. My parents were supportive of me and gave me a solid foundation. My older siblings provided good examples. I have been fortunate to have work that I found interesting and challenging. My faith has kept me grounded and my family has kept me fulfilled. The Irish have a long tradition of story-telling and it is with great relief that I know my story is accurately documented here so you can read it.

Epilogue

WHY DID I WRITE MY LIFE STORY?

It recently occurred to me during a chat session with several of my children that they knew very little of my early life story, outside of the highlights of the jobs I have held, places I have lived, and schools that I attended. I wanted to leave them a decidedly richer view into my past; one they might want to leave for their children and for later generations.

It was practical to only chronicle the highlights of my experiences without getting lost in the detail. For example, Ireland is intertwined in my story but would require an excessive number of pages to cover my many visits spanning 60 or so years. By the way, all four of my grandparents were born in County Clare, Ireland, and four of our five children have visited at least once. I also could not reasonably cover all of my other travels in depth since I have been to all of the fifty United States and all of the continents except Antarctica.

While working on this, I realize that I have documented certain aspects of a life style that many today would not understand. My mother never drove a vehicle other than a horse-drawn buggy. I would bet that most of my progeny couldn't tell the difference between a farm wagon, a spring wagon, or the many varieties of buggies. At age 92, I have provided my first-hand experiences in describing a world that no longer exists.

CPSIA information can be obtained
at www.ICGtesting.com
Printed in the USA
LVHW031803220223
740175LV00001B/6

9 780996 434980